I0396664

Coaching

Effective Coaching: How To Become A Coach Who Can Create Champions In Any Area Of Life

Steve Gold

<u>Table of Contents</u>

<u>Introduction</u>

When it comes to getting the best out of life - whether in your own life or from your team, there is no doubt that good coaching can play a pivotal role. Getting it right is about learning how to motivate yourself and others in a way that works. It means listening to yourself and others rather than just speaking at them. The good coach knows that they may not have all the answers.

In this book, we will teach you the basic elements of coaching to help you take your performance, and, where applicable, that of your team or others around you, to the next level. We will work on knowing what questions to ask, how to set accountability goals and how to ensure that the process is effective. You will learn not only how to ask the right questions but also how to listen to the answers given.

Good coaching is a simple and cost-effective way to zero in on what is important within your personal life and your business life. With the right encouragement, yourself and your team can go from muddling by to excelling and, after having read this book, you will know exactly how to provide the necessary support and encouragement.

Ready to skyrocket to success?

Chapter 1

Establishing Yourself as a Coach

When it comes to coaching – whether you are dealing with yourself or others, it is important to establish yourself as a trustworthy coach. This may seem a little strange – after all, surely after you've read this book you'll simply be able to call yourself a coach? Actually, it is a little more complicated than that.

As a coach, if you hope to get the best out of yourself and others, you'll need to create a more nurturing environment – you'll need to create an environment that fosters trust and respect if you hope for your efforts to bear fruit and lead to succeed.

When Coaching Yourself

Believe it or not, it is usually hardest to create this kind of nurturing environment when it comes to self-development. Think about it for a second – who is the person that you are hardest on? How many times do you criticize yourself for mistakes that you have made? Are you as hard on your team or those around you as you are on yourself? I seriously doubt it.

We have a tendency to be especially critical when it comes to ourselves – even when we make mistakes that we would readily forgive in others. You need to break out of that cycle if you want to up your game.

You need to be a non-judgmental mentor for yourself and this means actively stopping the constant self-critique. Every time you catch yourself wanting to self-chastise, you need to stop and give yourself a break. Take a step back from the situation and look at it objectively – if a friend or colleague made the same mistake, what would you tell them?

Whilst we do need to do some self-analysis in order to be able to grow, constant negative reinforcement will only erode our self-confidence and leave us fearful of taking the risks needed in order to grow.

When Coaching a Team

When it comes to coaching a team, you need to understand that there is a difference between talking *at* your team and working *with* them to help them improve. I used to work for a large company and I remember being required to attend many "coaching" sessions. Some were quite motivating, but what I remember most is that in all events, we had people telling us what to do. Never once were we asked what we thought.

Needless to say, the positive effects of these training sessions were short-lived. In addition to this, we were subjected to intensive "coaching" in order to improve sales. What this amounted to was having to submit sales figures twice a day and attending a meeting once a week, which in reality boiled down to being "name and shame" sessions. Our regional manager's style of motivation involved telling us that if we didn't like it, we knew where the door was!

Needless to say, all that these sessions accomplished was to make the attendees miserable. No one felt that they could raise issues they were facing for fear of being told that they were trying to make excuses, and consequently staff turnover was high.

In the long run, this kind of negative coaching costs organizations a lot in terms of a reduction in productivity and a greater cost in hiring and training – and then all of the money spent on training an individual went to waste when they inevitably left!

If, on the other hand, the regional manager had of worked on building trust with the staff and creating a positive environment, the rewards in terms of innovation and productivity would have been tangible. Instead of being the name and shame sessions they were, these could have been productive, problem-solving sessions.

Whether you are coaching a team or coaching yourself, it is important that you respect the individual or individuals and foster an environment that facilitates growth and development rather than one that is based on negative, competitive elements.

Knowing What You Want, to Get What You Want

Before you even set out on the path of coaching, it is important to establish what it is that you are aiming for. You need to set measurable and clearly defined goals. A lot of people just charge into coaching without having a clearly defined goal and end up being dissatisfied with the results.

By establishing what you want to achieve, and defining it clearly, you are giving yourself a much better chance of succeeding – you can then tailor your plan to your specific objectives and will be able to monitor your success against clear milestones as you progress.

For example, let us say that you want to improve sales in your organization. That is a pretty broad goal, and frankly one that is easily met – all you need is one extra sale and your goal is met. Because it is such a nebulous goal, you are bound to meet with mediocre results.

On the other hand, if you set a clear target of increasing the sales of a particular product by 10%, you are much more likely to be able to succeed because you have set a clearly definable goal.

Chapter 2

Learning to Listen Empathetically

The primary key, when it comes to coaching is to learn to listen empathetically to what others are saying. This is more than just listening to what they are saying – you also need to try and put yourself in the other person's shoes and really try to understand where they are coming from.

Drawing on my corporate experience again, I remember many sales meetings where we were talked at. We were asked what we thought and often asked for our opinions but it never seemed to make any difference. If you did not toe the company line, your input was ignored.

Unfortunately, this type of bullying, because in essence, that is what it is, is something that is viewed as being what a "no-nonsense" boss should aspire to. In reality though, all that you are doing is dampening morale and instilling a culture of fear in the organization. Initially, it may seem to work – staff do not want to be on the receiving end of this "motivational" tactic and may try harder as a result. But you better believe, the first chance they get they will be out of the door and you will have to start all over again.

Fortunately, listening with empathy is a skill that everyone can learn and it is not as difficult as you might think. Start by imagining yourself in the same situation as the person you are aiming to coach – what it is like to have to do what they are doing? What are their hopes and aspirations,? What cultural background do they have, etc.?

Using a simple cultural example – in the States, if someone seems to avoid your gaze, you may think that they are shifty or lying. In other cultures, such as the Zulu culture in South Africa, however, it is considered rude to stare directly into someone's eyes.

Now, let us imagine that you had an employee that believed it was rude to stare directly into your eyes - how would you react if you did not understand the cultural differences?

While this example may be overly simplistic in our complicated society, understanding where your mentee is coming from will pay great dividends when it comes to finding ways to motivate them successfully. And this empathetic listening pays great dividends when it comes to *any* form of coaching – whether in the office or on the sports field.

Understanding Where Your Team Members Are Coming From

Learning as much as possible about your employees as you can will be the first step in learning what makes them tick. If they say something that you don't understand from your own perspective, do ask them to explain further – getting them to explain the reasons behind why they offered that opinion makes it a lot easier to improve understanding between the two of you.

When learning about them, try to focus on things that you have in common with one another as opposed to differences and you are on your way to promoting a better understanding between the two of you.

Showing That You Are Empathetic

Start off by being completely sincere and pay complete attention when your mentee is speaking. So often we are so busy thinking of what our response is going to be that we actually miss out on the nuances of the conversation.

Show that you have heard and understood them by responding to what they said – picking up phrases that they used can be a good way to also demonstrate that you were listening.

Be guided by your mentee's body language – subtle mirroring of their body language gives them a greater impression that you are understanding what they are saying and will encourage them to continue.

Never interrupt your mentee, even to ask a question as it will break their train of thought and could be harmful to the process.

Chapter 3

Learning What Questions to Ask as a Coach

Coaching is going to require that you ask a number of questions, the skill is to do so in a way that it does not come across as an interrogation. Generally speaking, there are three types of questions that you will find useful and we will cover each of these in detail in this chapter:

- Curious Questions

- Clarifying Questions

- Possibility Questions

With an arsenal of these questions at your disposal, you will find that getting the information and responses that you require from those you are mentoring will be a lot easier. The main key with getting these questions right is to phrase them in a non-judgmental way, a way that is going to build the relationship and trust rather than destroy it. For example, "Why did you let the whole team down?" is question that is bound to illicit a defensive response because it seems accusatory. A better approach would be, "What went wrong on the project?"

Curious Questions

When it comes to curious questions, you need to be particularly careful in their phrasing or they may come off as accusatory. Curious questions start off with the following:

* How?

* What?

- Why?

- When?

- Supposing?

Curious questions should always be:

- Short and sweet – keep it to a maximum of 10 words.

- Concisely stated – Within the word count allowed, do ensure that you make it clear what you want answered.

- No "Yes" or "No" answers – leave the question open-ended to allow your mentee to expand upon their answer and explain their reasons more fully. This will help you to empathize with them better. You may also find that looking at things from a whole new angle sheds interesting light on the situation.

Now that you understand the basics of what your curious questions should be, it is time to talk a little on the phrasing of the questions.

As mentioned above, the last thing that you want to do is to put the person on the defensive so do take some time to compose the questions before you set them. If your mentee is on the defensive, they will keep looking for ways to justify their actions/ answers and this will not help anyone come to a better solution.

For example, "Why are you always so late getting to work?" is going to put your employee on the defensive immediately. On the other hand, you could say, "What reasons would you attribute to a delay in getting to work?" In both cases you are asking the same thing but the second question is a softer approach.

Think about the question before you ask it and view it from your employees point of view – how would you react if you were them? Be creative when phrasing your questions.

During the conversation that ensues, empathetic listening comes into play. Pick up on a phrase or two in the answers and build upon that in the next question. That way, you get more of the information that you want without coming across as an inquisitor.

Do set this session at a time when you have enough time to devote to it. You must ask no more than one question at a time and be able to consider the responses given and your own responses as well.

Also, be careful that you do not go into too much detail explaining your question or give hints as to what answers you were hoping to get – you want honest answers, not what the mentee is hoping you want to hear.

Also be careful about how you react to the answers given – even when you don't agree with them. If you get defensive when issues are brought up, your mentee will no longer feel comfortable raising issues with you. If, on the other hand, you demonstrate some empathy, your mentee will be encouraged to raise more issues, allowing you to get to the heart of the problem.

Clarifying Questions

It would be great if we could just ask the right curious questions and get all our answers that way. Unfortunately, in the real world, it just does not work that way. There are going to be times when you will need more details – where perhaps the mentee has not explained themselves properly or you do not fully understand the answer or where you need them to provide more details. For these times, clarifying questions are vital.

The aim here is to clarify what you have been told. For example, "Am I to understand that the bus service in your area is very unreliable?" You could also take this opportunity to ask more probing questions. For example, "Is it possible to find an alternate means to get to work?"

Again, the aim here is to ask questions that are more open-ended. By this stage in the conversation, however, you should have built up some trust so you can afford to be a little more direct. (Whilst still taking care not to put the person on the defensive.) Focus on the issue at hand rather than the person when formulating your clarifying questions.

Possibility Questions

If you want the mother-load of information, possibility questions are the best way to get it. The aim here is to get more information and perhaps to lead your mentee in the direction of coming up with a solution. For example, you could ask when training should start. By making them consider and give input on the possibilities, you automatically make it easier for them to buy in to the solution as well because they helped to come up with it.

So yes, again here we want open-ended questions but we do want to take a more targeted approach. Let's look at the question, "When should training start?". Whilst it is a valid question, it is not targeted enough – you could end up discussing the matter all day.

A better question would be, "Should we start training by the 15th, or is that too early?"

Now whilst your mentee could basically give any answer to the possibility questions posed to them, you can get a more targeted approach by steering the question properly. And by this I mean giving some guidelines in terms of the scope of the answer – not trying to make them give you the answer that you want.

The most useful aspect of possibility questions is that they can encourage your mentee to come up with the solution on their own, seemingly without your interference. This can make a great deal of difference when it comes to actually being able to implement the solution as mentees will think it was their idea.

There are a couple of ways to drive the conversation – you could pose the question and give a few possible solutions or you could pose the question and give the options of different answers.

For example, "Would you like to sign up now or do you want some time to talk to your family about it?"

When it comes to possibility questions be guided by your mentee and what you know about them – if they are prone to over-analyze things, apply stricter targeting; if they are hard to draw into conversation, apply a looser rein.

Chapter 4

Defining Successful Coaching

Ask ten people what a good coach is and you are likely to get ten different answers. For the most part, though, we judge the coach on the results that they achieve. That said though, there are a range of traits that you have to develop if you want to be a top notch coach.

You Need to be Patient and Persevere

Sometimes you will be able to break through to someone at the first meeting but this is generally the exception rather than the norm. You need to accept that the coaching process can be a slow one – you need to gain your mentee's trust before you can make real strides forward and this might be easier said than done at times.

It is also going to mean, at times, explaining things over and over again to people who just don't get it. If you cannot do this without losing your cool, you will need to work on yourself a bit before starting to coach others.

You also need to be willing to see things through –
even when it seems as though your mentee is making
very little progress. You never know when that final
breakthrough might occur and you do not want to
miss it.

If your mentee sees that you give up with only a little
effort, they will believe that they are not worth the
effort and that it is not worthwhile to try and
persevere in life in general.

Accept that, no matter how good you are at coaching,
there are going to be some mentees that learn fast and
others that don't – learn to tailor your approach and
patience accordingly.

You Need the Respect and Trust of Your Mentees

For coaching to be successful, your mentees need to respect you as a person and trust you as well. Note, I did not say that they had to like you – you do not have to be the drinking buddy that staggers home with them after a night out. You do, however, have to be there for them when you say you will be.

There is a saying, "Talk the talk and walk the walk". You need to lead by example and show your mentees that you actually live by the principles that you are teaching them. Let's say, for example, that you are a football coach and you have been drumming into your athletes the importance of eating right and not smoking. How much credibility will you have left if you walk onto the field with a cigarette in one hand a chili-cheese fries in the other?

The same goes for emotional coaching as well. Let us say, for example, that you are teaching your mentees about the importance of being patient. Afterwards you go to the store and start fuming about how long the line is and how slow the cashiers are – if one of your mentees were to see you, how much credibility would you lose?

Fair or not, when you are coaching others to improve themselves, you have to hold yourself at a higher standard and you really do have to practice what you preach in a consistent manner.

If your mentees know that you are there for them when you say that you will be, that you follow through on promises and that you are fair, they will start to trust and respect you.

As a coach, your goal is to get them to respect and trust you enough that they want to follow your advice or even aspire to be like you.

You Need to be Supportive

This is one of those common-sense skills but it is amazing how many coaches actually forget about it, especially as time goes by. Being supportive means taking the good with the bad and not being judgmental about it. You need to create a safe space so that your mentee knows that, even if they screw up, they can discuss it with you and they need to know that they can safely raise issues with you.

It's a bit like having a best friend who is dating someone that you really dislike. You might mention something to your friend but you generally end up tolerating the significant other for your friend's sake. Should they break up, you are there to support your friend and, if you are a good friend, to bite back on the, "I told you so".

In the end, a good coach points the mentee in the right direction but the mentee needs to make the final decision about what to do. They need to know that you will support them either way.

You Need to be a Subject Matter Expert

At least in part – you cannot teach people something that you yourself do not know. For example, it would be a little silly to take over coaching a baseball team when you know nothing about the game.

Now, that does not mean that you need to know everything about the job that your mentee is doing but it does mean that you need to know the techniques that you will be teaching backwards and forwards.

You need to be able to show your mentee how to adapt these techniques to suit themselves and how to apply them in different situations.

You Need to Have a Plan and a Contingency Plan

Jumping straight into coaching without doing any planning drastically reduces your chances of success. Work out a rough idea of what you will be covering and when and review periodically in terms of the progress that your mentee is making. Once you get to know your mentee better, it becomes easier to make decisions on the fly but until you get to that point, you better have a plan in place and a Plan B as well.

You Need to Be Able to Monitor Performance Against Specific Measurables

You as a coach do need to set up two sets of accounting systems – one for yourself and one for your mentee. Find ways to measure ongoing progress so that you can see whether or not your coaching style has been effective or not.

Also set up measurable goals for your mentees so that you are able to see whether or not they are progressing. These goals will also help to inspire them to perform better.

The Ability to Get People to Think for Themselves

In the past, coaching generally meant telling people what they needed to do and how they needed to think. Research has shown that this method has only limited success. In one study, one group was told exactly what to eat in order to lose weight – they had no opportunity to discuss this and were not told why. The second group was treated differently, they were presented with information on how certain foods helped with weight loss, and the long-term consequences of not losing the weight. They were presented with the basic guidelines for a healthy diet but the choice of foods, etc. were left to them.

Guess which group did better. Contrary to what you might think, participants in both groups lost about the same amount of weight over a four-week period. The difference in the number of dropouts was significantly higher in the first group, however.

Interestingly enough, when a follow-up was done three months later, it was found that the second group had performed significantly better when it came to maintaining the weight loss and a healthier lifestyle.

If you can get people to look at the issues being tackled critically and get them to really understand the consequences of action or inaction, you should be able to leave them to make the right decision on their own.

And that is coaching gold right there – if your mentee has figured out for themselves that your answer is the right one and that it will benefit them, they are going to get behind the process and give their very best.

Some coaches get annoyed when they have mentees who constantly ask them why their way is better or why it works. I love those mentees because I know that I have gotten their attention. And, quite frankly, if you cannot explain why what you are proposing works and what the benefit for the mentee is, you are wasting your time.

For most of us, the, "What's in it for me" drive is the strongest motivating factor.

Chapter 5

Assigning Accountability

I briefly spoke about the importance of having a plan in place and having clear measurable targets to achieve for both you and your mentee. In this chapter we will go into these concepts in greater detail.

Plan to Win and to Fail

Yes, I know – we should be positive and plan for the win but the truth is that having a plan in place to deal with failure is actually a lot more useful. We think and hope that everything will go alright, but what if it does not? With any luck, you won't even need the plan but, if you do, it will be there for you to use.

Take a lesson from the banks during the sub-prime market scandal and subsequent crash of 2008. It was inconceivable that a large corporate like Lehman Brothers would collapse and so most businesses did not prepare for such an eventuality. PIMCO, on the other hand, spent some time formulating a plan of action should Lehman Brothers collapse. When

Lehman Brothers did collapse, PIMCO was one of the few companies that had planned for the eventuality and, as a result, they were able to save their clients a lot of money.

Planning to win is fairly simple, take your mentee's ultimate goal and their proposed timeline and break it down into small, manageable steps that will work for your mentee in terms of their current circumstances and personality. The ultimate goal is to make it as easy as possible for your mentee to build the skills and traits needed to succeed.

The tasks that you set should start out simple and build in terms of complexity and difficulty as your mentee progresses.

Planning to fail is a little less fun but just as important. Take a look at your overall plan and consider what might go wrong. What if your mentee fails their exam or doesn't win the key race? How will you recover your plan from there?

Set Timelines

I read somewhere once that a list of goals without a specific time frame to complete them in was no more than a wish list and this is very true. Part of your job as a coach is to encourage your mentee to reach their goals and this entails putting a very real timeline on things.

It is important, however, to ensure that the timeline is realistic and to do regular reviews to ensure that it remains realistic.

Accountability and Responsibility

This means setting guidelines in place to ensure that everyone understands what their role is and what they are meant to be doing. The mentee has to understand that achieving the improvement that they require is going to take some work and the coach has to understand that they have a responsibility to monitor the progress of the mentee.

Once you have formulated your plan to win, see what responsibilities will need to be assigned to the mentee and to yourself. Set yourself a timeline to review progress and to see how things are going.

Once you know what you will be tasking your mentee with, you need to set accountability for the tasks – i.e. What will your mentee need to do and when will they need to do it by?

As regards your overall plan and how you convey it to your mentee, a lot will depend on your mentee themselves. Are you going to need to lead them so that they can find their own answers? If so, it may not be the best bet to let them know the full plan outright. In this case, give them a broad overview of what you will be doing without going into too many specifics and assign them the first task.

Depending on your mentee, it may even be necessary to take this accountability a step further – perhaps they need to give you regular progress reports. Being accountable to someone else can be a really huge motivating factor. Take the Weigh Less meetings, for example. Once week the various groups get together and everyone gets up and weighs themselves in front of the whole group. This is an example of accountability – except that it is not just being accountable to one person but a whole group. It works because you do not want to let others down or be embarrassed. It can also work for those who are highly competitive.

Chapter 6

Reviewing Progress and Changing Course

Most people love the planning phase of things and think that, once that has been done, the hard work is over. Unfortunately, putting the plan into effect is only the first phase – you will need to do periodic reviews in order to ensure that the plan is actually effective and that things are going as planned.

When to Review

It seems to make sense that you set your reviews up just after the target date for goals so that you can see exactly how things went. This is a valid approach but it could be a case of too little too late. What if things are not working out as you planned? If you leave it until the target deadline is reached and only review it then, you have wasted time and probably demotivated your mentee to boot.

It is better to do a review at about a quarter of the way through, another at half, and a third, if necessary at three quarters of the way through. What I like to do, in addition, is to check with my mentee a few days after the program has been instituted to see how they are coping with the change.

This may sound like a lot of work in terms of reviews to be done but it is especially important when starting off with your mentee and should be continued with until you know for sure that they are coping with your style of motivation and coaching. If you switch up styles or try something new, go back to this regular reviewing schedule.

Some reviews are good, so more are even better right? Up to a point. Remember me talking about my experience working for a large corporate. We had to submit sales figures twice daily so that management could review our progress and had to go for a weekly sales meeting as well. The weekly meeting on its own would have been annoying but okay. Having to submit figures twice daily was not only an intrusion and waste of time but it had the opposite of the desired effect. The theory was that submitting the figures in this manner would motivate us more and lead to greater productivity – what it did, however, was sap morale and cause anxiety. Within 3 years, every single member of that sales team, me included, had left the company.

The system was scrapped soon thereafter because it was clear that it wasn't working. In the interim, however, they wasted three years simply because they didn't want to course correct.

What to Review

There is more to these reviews than just seeing how your mentee is progressing. You also need to touch base with them to see how things are going and how they are feeling about the progress that they are making.

Oftentimes we tend to look at success as the ultimate goal and ignore the journey that it takes to get there. You do need to ensure that you are not putting undue pressure on your mentee as you move forward and that their goals have not changed over time.

It's kind of like what we see played out over and over again – you have a young boy whose parents want the best for them. They want him to be a sports star, let's say in baseball so they hire him a trainer or make him practice every day after school, whether he wants to or not. If being a star baseball player is his dream as well, this could work out well for him. If it is not, he is going to end up being miserable and probably hating baseball and his parents to boot.

It is important to understand that what people want can also change over time. Again, using myself as an example, I decided early in my career that I wanted a management position within 5 years. (At the time, that was unheard of and everybody told me it was a pipe dream). I worked hard, I studied hard and I got myself onto an accelerated training program. I achieved my goal and became one of the youngest managers in the firm.

I was ecstatic, for about a week. Then I started to realize that the position was not all that I had hoped for. I stuck it out for another 4 years, all the while becoming more and more miserable. You see, over time, I had changed – I had achieved what I wanted to but because of this change, there was no satisfaction in it for me. Despite all the time spent studying and building my career, I decided that the time had come for me to resign and try something else. Again, everyone told me I was doing the wrong thing. Again, it turned out to be the best course of action for me.

If your mentee decides that they want to change direction, you need to try and support them in that decision.

Course Corrections in Need

There are times when you are going to come up with the most outstanding plan, one that simply cannot fail. One that you know will definitely succeed. You do your reviews as you go along but are not seeing the results that you feel that you should. It must be something that the mentee is doing wrong, mustn't it?

It's a tough one to accept but not every plan that we think is perfect is going to work out for our mentees. When it comes to the actual execution of the plan, things could go wrong and we need to accept this and move along, changing the plan as necessary.

Dealing with Failures

As a coach, it can be downright disheartening when you put your all into it and your mentee fails. It is tempting to blame them outright for the failure and let them know how badly they let you down. This is only going to damage the relationship that you have built and so you have to be really careful about how you deal with failures.

It also bears remembering that your mentee is probably just as disappointed and also feeling guilty for letting you down. How you deal with failures is just as instrumental in your mentee's ultimate success.

The first thing to do is to be as non-judgmental as possible and to try and ascertain why the plan failed. Speak to your mentee, asking curious questions such as, "What were the difficulties that you encountered." Make it clear that you are not making a personal attack but are just trying to find out what went wrong so that it doesn't happen again.

Once you have established what the problem was, you can tweak your plan so that you can prepare your mentee better in future.

Dealing with Successes

Of course, there will also be some successes along the way and it is important that you and your mentee do celebrate these as well. When setting up your plan, do make a note of how the two of you will celebrate successes. When speaking about the tasks or goals with your mentee, it can serve as good motivation to let them know what you are planning when they succeed.

It may seem odd, but successes may also call for a rethink of the overall plan. If you find that your mentee is progressing at a faster rate than expected, you might want to consider shortening the timeline – after discussing it with them, of course.

Whether you are course correcting due to success or failure, it is important to restart the reviewing process again – check in with your mentee to ensure that the new track is working for them and check back with them regularly.

Chapter 7

Dealing with Common Issues

If only we could wave a magic wand and make everything right with the world. Some people think that coaching their mentees will have a similar effect and then end up disappointed when things do not go quite as planned. Nothing in life is ever that simple, I'm afraid – you are going to face challenges as a coach. This chapter deals with some common issues that you may have to face and how to deal with them.

Lack of Commitment

You are going to come across some mentees who attend the coaching sessions and then just don't seem to want to do the work involved. This is usually when someone else has sent the mentee to be coached but can also happen when mentees hire a coach themselves.

A lack of commitment is not an insurmountable obstacle – you just need to find a way to show the mentee that the benefits of taking action (like practicing their piano playing for an extra hour a day) outweigh the benefits of not taking action (like getting to watch their favorite Netflix series). Once again, we have to come back to the, "What's in it for me?" part of the equation.

Get your mentee to list all the benefits of sticking to the coaching track. Get them to visualize success in their minds – the more vivid the picture the better. Get them to create a vision board so that they have a constant visual reminder of what they want to achieve to motivate them.

Procrastination

All of us, at one time or another, procrastinate. Procrastination is a particular problem when we are facing something that takes us out of our comfort zones or is a little more difficult. Coaches are bound to face a client that procrastinates to some degree.

Understanding why they procrastinate is essential if you want to help them get over it.

Generally speaking, there are two main reasons why we procrastinate (and, no, they are not laziness or lack of willpower) – fear of failure and fear of success. If your mentee is battling with procrastination, you need to delve deeper and find out what they fear will happen if they carry out the tasks.

If they fear failure, try and break the tasks into smaller and more easily attained goals so that they have some easy wins to build their confidence.

If they fear success – I know this sounds strange but many people fear the impact of success on their lives in terms of changed relationships and increasing responsibilities – you need to get to what the root of the fear is. What is it they think that they will lose by succeeding?

It may even be that your mentee has little to no conscious idea about what the problem is and you can help them using the following exercise introduced to us by Julia Cameron in her book, "The Artist's Way":

Every day your mentee needs to sit down and write until they have covered two full A4 sized pages. This should preferably be in the morning but afternoon will work if pressed for time. On these pages, your mentee can write whatever they like with one condition – there is no censorship, no worrying about correct phrasing, spelling or grammar and no rereading to check that it reads right. They write whatever comes to mind – no one else will read these pages.

When I first tried this exercise, I thought that it was stupid so I wrote, "This is stupid" over and over again for about a half a page. Then I thought, "This reminds me of the time ...." and suddenly I was writing about thinks that happened at school – things that I had completely forgotten about. I now do this exercise every morning.

Try it – you will be amazed at what comes up during these sessions.

Mentees Unable or Unwilling to Communicate

You are bound to get a few of these – you know the type – they stick to monosyllabic answers as far as possible and getting information out of them is like trying to find hen's teeth.

With these people, the route of the problem often stems from an inability to trust easily or a fear of being judged. The only way to solve this issue is to work on building trust – try sharing something about yourself and, when they do finally tell you something, make sure that you never interrupt them and be non-judgmental.

Here patience is especially important – it will take some time to build a relationship in this instance.

Mentees That Want to be Spoon-Fed

You will also come across some mentees that expect you to have all the answers and to do all the work for them. Dealing with these mentees can be frustrating as they are usually looking for a quick fix.

In this instance, it is important to conduct exercises that force them to be more self-reliant and to get them to become excited about the process so that they are more likely to proceed with it.

Mentees That Don't Know What They Want

Whilst you can supply some guidance here in helping them determine what they want out of life, they are going to have to do the heavy lifting here. Until they actually know what to aspire towards, coaching will be a rather one-sided process.

General Tips

If you are finding that you are having trouble with getting your mentee to move forward, there are several things that you can do.

- A coach/ mentee relationship should always be a partnership and not a power struggle. Your goal is to work with your mentee and to guide them, not to take over completely. Listen to what your mentee is telling and make sure that they know that you are really trying to understand where they are coming from.

- Be sincere or move on. You may not always like your mentee but you should always be sincere in your desire to help them. Because of the especial closeness of this relationship, your mentee will soon be able to see if you are a fake and will respond accordingly by not putting in a full effort. If you want to get into coaching purely for the money, you are looking at the wrong profession completely.

- Help them to visualize a successful outcome as imaginatively as possible. They need to not only be able to see what success looks like in their mind's eye but also how it will feel to be successful and how they will react to success.

- Start off with small, easy to reach goals. Starting off with small goals like this helps to give early wins that are necessary to build your mentee's confidence in the process and in your ability to guide them. Setting up difficult goals at the outset is more likely to lead them to give up. Let's say, for example, your mentee wants to lose 40 pounds. If you hand them a strict diet and tell them to exercise for an hour a day, how long will they stick to the program? If, on the other hand, you ask them to walk around the block every day and maybe start each meal with a piece of fruit, they are a lot more likely to be able to stick to the program.

- You need to keep the dialogue going – if things are not working out, ask your mentee why they think that this is – their feedback could be key to making this work.

- Try a different approach. If your mentee is achieving very little, it may be time to adjust your style of coaching more to their personality type. Try something a little more exciting or approach the matter from a completely new perspective to see if that helps.

- Admitting that you need help if you need it. As a coach, we like to think that we are equipped to deal with every situation. There may be times, however, when your mentee has something that you cannot help them with. A coach/ mentee relationship that has been built up properly will involve your mentee divulging personal details and this may mean that you may need to call in help. Say, for example, that your mentee tells you that they are having suicidal thoughts – are you equipped to help them with that? Whilst you can talk it through with them, it is also advisable to let them know that you are concerned and ask them if you can find them someone more qualified to deal with that issue.

- Constantly challenge yourself to learn more and to develop yourself as a person so that you are better able to assist your mentees. Coaching is a lifelong learning process – advances are constantly being made and you need to keep abreast of these as well. You don't have to confine yourself to books either, get out there and meet people of different cultures. Travel if you are able and do give yourself the chance to experience new things. Your coaching skills can only improve as a result.

Conclusion

Whether you are coaching yourself or coaching someone else, you now have the basic tools that you need to get started. Coaching someone and helping them to achieve their goals is an immensely rewarding experience and something that each and every one of us should do at least once in our lifetimes.

Possibly the best part of the experience for me is that you never really stop learning and improving yourself in the process. I am often amazed at the insights of some of the people that I coach and am fascinated by the different perspectives that I learn about.

Coaching is not always easy but there is nothing quite like knowing that you have helped someone else reach for their star. At the end of the day, you have everything to gain and little to lose.

All that's left for me to say now is that there is no time like the present for you to get out there and get started. Expect to make mistakes along the way and view them as learning experiences and you will soon find that you are a top class coach.

A message from the author,

Steve Gold

To show my appreciation for your support, Id like to

offer you a couple of exclusive free gifts:

FREE BONUS!

As a free bonus, I've included a preview of

some of my other best-selling books directly

after this section. Enjoy!

FREE BONUS!: Preview Of

"Leadership - The Keys to

Becoming a Person of

Influence in Business & in

Life"!

If you enjoyed this book, I have a little bonus for you;

a preview of one of my other books!

Chapter 2

Habits of Highly Effective Leaders

Great leaders are made, not born. In fact, effective leadership stems from the accumulation of good personal habits that foster certain qualities in an individual, enabling them to inspire and guide others to greater heights. In essence, anyone can learn to become a competent leader. It starts with a conscious decision to cultivate certain ways of thinking and doing things, which are then practiced until they become automated behaviors.

It Starts with You!

Before you have the capacity to competently lead others, you have to first be your own leader and take charge of your own life. As an example, let's look at the story of Carl the window cleaner:

50 year-old Carl is one of the custodians at a commercial building that housed some of the most prestigious law, tech and business firms in town. For more than a decade since he was employed, he has shown a consistent record of showing for work on-time almost every morning – save for the occasional family emergency and medical leave. Because he shows no fear for heights, he has been tasked to clean the large glass windows of the 20th floor. Every day,

like clockwork, Carl would clean the same windows three times; in the morning, after lunch and before heading home. He ensures the windows are spotless, because it is his job. He does this with an understanding of how important it is for the businesses that operate in the building to project a classy image to visitors. Carl's cleaning routine is so ingrained that he does not even have to think about it. Throughout the years, his work ethic has caught the attention of other custodians that then began emulating him.

Carl's story demonstrates what it is like to be one's own leader. He does not have a team of staff answering to him, neither is his job a glamorous one. However, Carl understands that he has a role to fulfill and a purpose to serve – as small as that purpose may be in the grand scheme of things. Hence, he took it upon himself to give it his very best every day on the job, leading by example and inspiring others to follow suit. Carl is therefore a leader.

The moral of the story is that regardless of your position on the corporate ladder – or where you are in life, for that matter – leadership skills will always serve you well.

The Personal Leadership Action Plan

By now, you should already have a basic idea of the qualities that account for good leadership. The key is to remember that becoming an effective leader is a choice, but it does involve action on one's part to cultivate the required habits and mindset.

Here is a blueprint of what you want to incorporate into your daily life when aspiring to be a better leader. Be sure to follow the simple thought exercises along the way. Spend some time to think about them, and consider jotting down your thoughts so as to make them more concrete. Also, feel free to revisit any of the points here later on, if needed.

1. Believe in and be passionate about what you do.

Effective leaders inspire others to follow along because they have a genuine passion and enthusiasm for what it is that they do. Their passion comes from the belief that they are adding value to the lives of others. If you feel that your job is insignificant and you are easily replaceable, it would help to adopt a "bigger picture outlook" and recognize that you have a service to offer.

Exercise

Consider your current job role and responsibilities. How does your job performance affect the organization's daily operations as a whole? If your job were to be removed, how would that impact the people (clients and customers) that the company serves?

2. Define your core values and live by them.

Have you ever made choices only for your decisions to have lead to a nagging feeling of unease you just couldn't shake off? You likely felt this way because you knew at the back of your mind that the decisions you made were against your core values and what you truly believed to be right.

When one's actions are at odds with their ethics, our subconscious becomes occupied with feelings of guilt and caution, hindering thoughts that are conducive to productivity and success in any endeavor. However, when our thoughts and actions are aligned with our personal values and ethics, our conscience remains clear. In addition, we will garner more trust from people when they sense integrity in our words and actions.

Exercise

Think back to a time where you made a decision or do something which you were not proud of, only for it to have haunted your conscience. Examine why it made you feel bad. Was it because you went against your personal code of ethics? Was someone or something compromised along the way? What would you have don't differently if you could go back and do it all over again? How could you make sure to not repeat this mistake again in future?

3. Maintain a positive outlook.

We do not always have control over what happens in our lives, but what we *always* have is control over how we chose to react to it. Someone with a positive outlook is always looking on the bright side of things. Furthermore, optimism is infectious, and people naturally want to be around those who lift their spirits when circumstances seem less than desirable.

Exercise

Think of at least one situation where you tried to accomplish a task, but the outcome did not turn out as well as you expected. What are the good things that came out of the situation? It could be an unexpected blessing in disguise, a lesson learned or a new discovery you were able to make.

4. Know your strengths and how to utilize them.

Everyone is good at something, whether it is a technical or soft skill. Perhaps you are more knowledgeable and experienced in certain subjects than others around you. Knowing how to harness your strengths gives you an edge over others, thus making you a valuable part of a team.

Exercise

What are the technical and soft skills that you have developed over your lifetime? You may have a technical skill, such as drawing, writing, or mathematics. Maybe you are good at keeping things organized, or perhaps you are a natural conversationalist. Make a list of your strengths and think of how they come in handy at work, and in your day-to-day life. Where could you be using your talents more fully?

5. Be willing to admit your weakness and learn from mistakes.

No one is perfect, and the most successful leaders are not afraid of failure – they humbly acknowledge their shortcoming and learn from their mistakes. One of the keys to effective and respectable leadership is the willingness for a leader to communicate their weaknesses, so that others who excel at particular tasks can be appointed to the team.

Exercise

You have listed your strengths, now list your weaknesses. For the weakness that you have listed, what can you do to minimize or improve upon them?

Recall a time where your weaknesses resulted in a less than desirable outcome for an assigned task. If such circumstances were to reoccur, how would you have handled them differently?

6. Learn to show, not tell.

The best leaders are those who walk the talk. You cannot inspire admiration and respect without being able to back up your claims with proactive actions.

Exercise

What value do you believe you bring to the team or company? What would you like your team or co-workers to improve upon? How can you work on modeling those qualities yourself, on a daily basis?

Check out the rest of "Leadership - The Keys to Becoming a Person of Influence in Business & in Life" on Amazon.

Check Out My Other Books!

Elon Musk - The Biography Of A Modern Day Renaissance Man

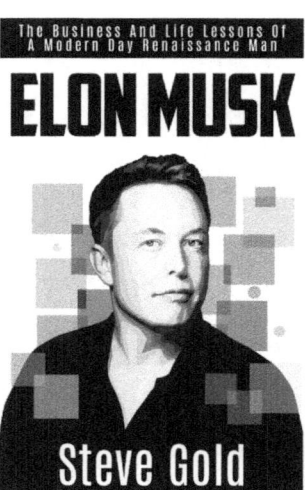

Elon Musk - The Business & Life Lessons Of A Modern Day Renaissance Man

Warren Buffett - The Business And Life
Lessons Of An Investment Genius, Magnate
And Philanthropist

Steve Jobs - The Biography & Lessons Of The
Mastermind Behind Apple

Management - Achieve Management Excellence & World Class Leadership Skills In 7 Simple Steps

Sales - Easily Sell Anything To Anyone & Achieve Sales Excellence In 7 Simple Steps

**Arduino - Getting Started With Arduino: The
Ultimate Beginner's Guide**

All books available as ebooks or printed books